TONY EVANS

THE FIRE THAT IGNITES

LIFECHANGE BOOKS

Multnomah Books

THE FIRE THAT IGNITES
published by Multnomah Books
© 2003 by Tony Evans

International Standard Book Number: 978-1-60142-438-9
Cover design by Kirk DouPonce/UDG—DesignWorks

Cover image by Gary Rhijnsburger/Masterfile
Italics in Scripture quotations are the author's emphasis.

Unless otherwise indicated, Scripture quotations are from:
The Holy Bible, English Standard Version
© 2001 by Crossway Bibles,
a division of Good News Publishers.

Other Scripture quotations are from:
The Holy Bible, New International Version (NIV) © 1973, 1984 by International Bible Society,
used by permission of Zondervan Publishing House. *The Holy Bible,* King James Version (KJV).
The Holy Bible, New King James Version (NKJV) © 1984 by Thomas Nelson, Inc.

Published in the United States by WaterBrook Multnomah, an imprint of the
Crown Publishing Group, a division of Random House Inc., New York.

MULTNOMAH and its mountain colophon are registered trademarks of Random House Inc.

Printed in the United States of America

For information:
MULTNOMAH BOOKS
12265 ORACLE BOULEVARD, SUITE 200 • COLORADO SPRINGS, CO 80921

Library of Congress Cataloging-in-Publication Data

Evans, Anthony T.
    The fire that ignites / by Tony Evans.
        p. cm.
    ISBN 1-59052-083-1
    1. Holy Spirit. 2. Spiritual life—Christianity. I. Title.
BT121.3.E93 2003
231'.3—dc21

                                                              2003006575

CONTENTS

Chapter 1

MORE OF THE SUPERNATURAL

Pretend with me for a moment that you need a new refrigerator. You walk into an appliance store one afternoon and quickly spot the one you want—their most expensive model, naturally, with all the bells and whistles. The shelves even slide out automatically when you open the door. This is the real thing, the refrigerator for the twenty-first century.

You buy it for ten thousand dollars, and they promise to deliver it that very day.

On your way home, you stop at a food market and buy plenty of groceries. And you've just carried the last bag into the kitchen when the delivery men arrive. They bring your shiny new appliance inside and set it in its place, and you immediately stock it full with all the wonderful food you've purchased. That night you fall asleep thinking of delicious meals to come.

The next morning, you go eagerly to the kitchen and open your refrigerator's door. But the shelves do not come gliding out automatically; they just sit there. What's worse, melted ice cream in the freezer section has run down and is all over everything. The vegetables are turning color, and you discover that the milk has gone sour.

It dawns on you that your top-of-the-line refrigerator is not functioning as you were led to believe it would.

You grab the phone, call the appliance store, and ask to be connected with the salesperson who sold you the merchandise. When he answers, you give him a piece of your evangelical Christian mind.

"Look," you say, "I gave you ten thousand dollars, and you sold me a lemon."

The salesman is stupefied. "Well," he says earnestly, "will you please go and open the refrigerator door again and then tell me if the light comes on."

You step over and open it. No light.

"Well, do me a favor," the salesman continues. "Would you put your ear down at the bottom where the motor is, and tell me if you hear a hum?"

You bend over and listen. No hum.

"Now then," the salesman says, "if you don't mind, would you kindly look around the back of the refrigerator and check to see if the cord is plugged in tight?"

You go and look behind the refrigerator. The end of the cord is lying there, loose on the floor.

You get back on the phone. "I checked—and the cord hasn't been plugged in. But for ten thousand dollars, that shouldn't matter. For ten thousand dollars, it ought to work just on general principle!"

Bought a Lemon?

That's when the salesman gently clarifies something for you. Appliances, he explains, are intricately designed to have astounding capabilities. They are, however, dependent in nature. While they have all the component parts needed to perform everything the manufacturer designs each appliance to do, they aren't able to accomplish this on their own. They first need to be empowered by the fire that electricity provides. Only then can the parts do what the parts were created to do.

When you and I gave our lives to Jesus Christ, He gave us new parts. He gave us a new mind, a new heart, a new conscience, and a new disposition. He granted us a whole new nature inside our existing body. It was like new residents moving into an old house.

But sometimes it looks like this new thing doesn't work. Sometimes it appears that coming to Christ is like buying a lemon—it just doesn't seem to function the way

> Sometimes it appears that coming to Christ is like buying a lemon.

we were led to believe it would.

That's why you and I must clearly understand that we're dependent by nature. We were never re-created in Christ to function on our own. We need power; we need enabling from another source to ignite the proper functioning of the new nature God has provided us.

In this book we'll see how the Holy Spirit—the third member of the triune God—makes the power and the promises of God experiential in the life of every believer. All that God has said, all that He has promised, all that He has granted and given and graced us with—all of this "works" only when we're fully connected to the one source of enabling, God's Holy Spirit.

It's my hope that by the time you finish this book, you'll know where the socket is…and that you will in fact be plugged in.

EXPERIENCING THE SUPERNATURAL

Now of course in our houses we have a number of appliances besides a refrigerator, and they all do different work; they each have a unique function. But for power, they all depend on the same source, electricity.

Likewise, you and I are unique in the new identity and

giftedness God has designed for each of us as believers, and the same is true for all our brothers and sisters in Christ. In the church we've got toaster Christians, can-opener Christians, dishwasher Christians, and coffeemaker Christians. But we all plug into the same power, the same enabler. And when we do, it means we become what we're created to become in our new identity in Christ.

The Holy Spirit has been given to every Christian and to the corporate family of God to make real *in your own spiritual experience* everything the Bible says. The job of the Holy Spirit is to lift this truth off the pages of Scripture and write it on your heart—making it *alive,* making it vivid. And that means leading you into a whole new realm of existence. It means experiencing the supernatural.

Why then aren't more of us experiencing the supernatural? In our churches and in our families and in our personal lives, why aren't more of us seeing the supernatural invasion of God—more of His wind, more of His fire?

In the pages ahead we'll look carefully into God's Word and at our lives to answer that question. For now, it's enough to say that if any Christian is defeated or powerless, that Christian is defeated or powerless not because he has to be, but because he is either uninformed or has chosen to be powerless. For the provision and presence of the Holy Spirit is God's unfailing promise, poured out upon us to link us to the very reality of God Himself.

A CHANGE IN THE POWER EQUATION

Think intently about that for a moment—about the Holy Spirit as our link to God's reality, His power.

You know what it's like to be stranded in a parking lot somewhere with a dead battery in your car. You're in trouble, and you seek assistance. When some helpful friend or stranger responds, they park alongside your stranded vehicle. With the hoods opened on both cars, a set of jumper cables is attached to both batteries, linking them. Then the other person starts the ignition in his car.

What happens next is a transfer of power. Through the cables, power from the living battery is transferred to the dead one. One battery borrows life from another...so that the dead battery becomes as alive as the living battery already is.

But for all that to happen, there must first be a connection.

The basic, underlying situation for every human being on earth is that we're in trouble, stranded. We need life inside our dead battery to give us the ability to become all God wants us to become.

Jesus is our friend who comes to the rescue. And the Holy Spirit is our set of jumper cables; His job is to connect our life with Christ's life, allowing a transfer of His life to ours. And then we experience the secret of life and power—"which is Christ in you, the hope of glory" (Colossians 1:27).

The Holy Spirit changes the power equation in our lives. He changes the ability equation, because what He provides is supernatural life from Christ himself, equipping and empowering us so completely that we can never again say we lack the ability to do what He calls us to do.

To Know and to Treasure

In many ways, the Holy Spirit is like the "lost member" of the Trinity. Some people admit they just don't understand Him. Others profess to know Him well—while revealing their true ignorance by what they say and do.

And yet the Holy Spirit is actually the person of the Trinity who's most actively *with* us now. And He's indispensable to your Christian life and mine. If there were no Holy Spirit, there would be no gospel, no faith, no church—no Christianity at all. In fact, our world and our universe would not even exist, for Genesis 1 shows the Spirit of God "hovering" over the original creation.

If there were no Holy Spirit, there would be no human life, for God breathed, or spirited, into Adam the breath of life (Genesis 2:7).

If there were no Holy Spirit, there would have been no virgin birth of Jesus, for Mary became preg-

> The Spirit is the person of the Trinity who's most actively with us now.

nant by the "overshadowing" of the Holy Spirit (Matthew 1:20; Luke 1:35).

If there were no Holy Spirit, there would be no Bible, because those who wrote it "spoke from God as they were carried along by the Holy Spirit" (2 Peter 1:21).

If there were no Holy Spirit, there would be no victory over Satan, no restraint of sin, no dispensing of grace for salvation, no victory in our trials, no second coming of Jesus Christ, and no participation for us in the coming kingdom of our Lord. To live the Christian life without the Holy Spirit's active participation is absolutely impossible. The same goes for being a church that God blesses—without the active, dynamic involvement of the Holy Spirit, it's absolutely impossible.

The Holy Spirit of God is more vital and essential to our life and faith than most of us have ever imagined…and that's why it's so imperative that we learn more about Him.

In this book we'll explore the person of the Spirit, His presence with us, and His purpose and His provisions for us. We'll also focus especially on what it means in our lives to be filled with the Spirit—because that's the only way we can consistently experience and enjoy the supernatural.

I want to help you study closely the promises God makes to us concerning His Spirit so you can know and treasure these truths enough to make a lasting difference in your life.

Chapter 2

ANOTHER DIMENSION, ANOTHER REALITY

There was a woman whose husband died unexpectedly after several happy years of marriage. She couldn't bear the thought of life without John, so she had him embalmed and brought him back home.

Every morning she propped up John in his familiar easy chair and chatted with him, just as she always had before. "What would you like to do today, dear?" she would ask. She turned on the TV to his favorite programs; she brought out his favorite meals on a tray.

The time came when she needed to travel to another part of the country to handle some business, and while she was away, she met Bill. She fell in love with Bill, and after a whirlwind romance she married him and brought him back home with her.

As they walked arm in arm into the house, Bill suddenly stopped cold in his tracks.

"What's that?" he asked his bride.

"Oh," she answered, "that's John, my old husband."

For a long, silent moment, Bill looked from one to the other. Then he declared, "Well, honey, you're going to have to make a choice...."

DEAD WAS DEAD

That's what it basically comes down to for us as well. Will we choose to devote ourselves entirely to Someone who's alive and can bring us vitality and victory and fruitfulness and freedom? Or will we keep trying to hold on to our old existence—something that's dead and ought to be buried?

Don't forget what was true of all of us before we came to Christ: "As for you, *you were dead* in your transgressions and sins" (Ephesians 2:1, NIV). Though physically alive, we had no ability back then to know or understand or communicate with God.

We were like the walking dead in those old horror movies. We went about working, eating, marrying, going here, going there—but we were dead. Some of us were good-looking and dead; others were ugly and dead. Some were rich and dead; some poor and dead. Some were quiet and bashful and dead, while others were bold and outspoken and dead. But we were all spiritually lifeless, without any connection to God or any true God-awareness—that was our condition. Our spirits were dead.

And *dead* means "dead."

I have a mortician friend who told me that as he's doing his work, sometimes the corpse will have muscular contractions. A hand will quiver, a face will twitch, an eye will blink. He calmly recounted how he once saw a corpse jerk so violently that it almost lifted itself off the table and onto the floor. (If I'd been there and seen that, it would have meant *two* corpses falling to the floor!)

I asked my friend, "Don't those things disturb you?"

"Absolutely not."

"Why?"

"Because," he answered, "dead is dead."

Dead is what we all were, spiritually speaking. But the Holy Spirit is "the Spirit of *life*" (Romans 8:2); "the Spirit who *gives* life" (John 6:63). When He saved us, the Spirit immersed us into another dimension, another reality—the

> We were like the walking dead in those old horror movies.

realm of spiritual aliveness. We're so alive now that we leave death behind forever, just as Jesus did when He rose from the grave (Romans 6:3–4).

BAPTISM IN THE SPIRIT

This miraculous life-giving immersion is called our "baptism" in the Spirit—"For in one Spirit we were all baptized into one body" (1 Corinthians 12:13). It's what we all experienced at the time of our salvation.

Spiritually speaking, there's no such thing as a non-baptized Christian; you don't get saved one day and get baptized later in the Spirit. "We were *all* baptized," Paul told the Corinthians—even though he reprimanded them for being "still worldly" (1 Corinthians 3:3, NIV), "still carnal" (NKJV). They weren't yet mature as believers, but they had indeed been Spirit-baptized. Baptism in the Spirit is a universal reality for Christians.

We get this word *baptize* from a Greek term meaning "to dip." It was used for the work of a dyer of cloth—he would dip cloth in dye to recolor it, giving it a new and different identity. He was a baptizer.

When God's Holy Spirit baptizes us at the time of our salvation, Jesus is the "dye" that we're immersed in. We're "baptized *into* Christ Jesus" (Romans 6:3), and out of that baptism we rise up new and different. We're the same person, but with a totally new identity. We're now the color of Christ.

That color is as bright as light itself. When you were outside of Christ, you were in the dark. Satan, the prince of darkness, was your father, and you belonged to him and obeyed him even when you didn't know it. But when you were baptized by the Spirit of God, you were "rescued...from the dominion of darkness" and transferred into the Father's "kingdom of light" (Colossians 1:12–13).

Baptism in the Spirit is therefore a cataclysmic event: It activates a whole new sphere of dynamic existence for us, the living environment of Christ Himself. We're in an entirely new actuality, a different kingdom, where we answer to a new king.

A NEW ONENESS

By the way, the featured point in Scripture of the Spirit's baptism is that it brings people from different backgrounds together into one family. Notice again Paul's words: "For in one Spirit we were all baptized into one body—Jews or Greeks, slaves or free—and all were made to drink of one Spirit" (1 Corinthians 12:13). *One, one, one.* This supernatural, superinclusive unity is a fact, not some lofty but unrealistic ideal, and our failure to accept this spiritual fact and to live

> Baptism in the
> Spirit is a
> cataclysmic
> event.

it out is a grievous insult to the Spirit.

Real unity is further from us than we sometimes think. My wife and I have been turned away from two churches because of the color of our skin. Discrimination by race as well as by class and cultural background still exists in the church, sometimes overtly, sometimes behind the scenes, and wherever this corruption occurs, the power of the Spirit will always be suppressed.

HE COMES TO STAY

When we believe in Christ and the Holy Spirit baptizes us, He also *indwells* us. He does exactly as Jesus promised when He explained "the Spirit of truth" to His disciples: "You know him, for he dwells with you and will be in you" (John 14:17).

Inside your inner self, there is *Him*—not a mere substance or stimulation or some Star Wars "force," but an actual person who expresses His life within you. One of our major mistakes today in understanding the Holy Spirit is to miss that He's a real person. We want to relate to Him only as a power supply or a glorified energy field, rather than growing in our personal relationship with Him. He's a person to be known, not simply a power to be used.

But we get thrown for a loop because He's spirit, and we must relate with Him spiritually. We aren't used to that kind of person—a spirit-person—except maybe in movies. Being *spirit* means he's nonmaterial, beyond our five senses.

We don't directly touch Him in a physical sense, or see Him or smell Him or hear Him. That's why Jesus said that the world "neither sees him nor knows him" (John 14:17). He's vitally real, but He must be spiritually perceived.

And yet He's alive with intellect, and with emotions, and with a will of His own—the same three characteristics all persons have.

He thinks with incredible wisdom and intelligence, because "the Spirit searches everything, even the depths of God" (1 Corinthians 2:10).

The Holy Spirit has feelings; in fact, He's very sensitive emotionally, and that's why we're commanded, "Do not grieve the Holy Spirit of God" (Ephesians 4:30).

> The Holy Spirit
> has feelings; He's
> very sensitive
> emotionally.

And with His will, He makes choices and decisions—as for

example when He told the church at Antioch to "set apart for me Barnabas and Saul for the work to which I have called them" (Acts 13:2).

Being a person also means He's complete and indivisible. Some people say, "Our problem is that we need more of the Holy Spirit." But the issue is never how much of the Holy Spirit you have, because He's inside you and that means *all* of Him. No, the real question is this: How much of *you* does the Holy Spirit have? How much are you letting Him fill you and control you? (We'll explore that a lot more later.)

So by the miracle-working power of God, this amazing person is no longer external from you, but internal. And He came to stay. You're indwelt permanently, in perpetuity. There's no cause ever again to feel "far" from God—because how far can you get from your own insides?

His Anointing

Sometimes Christians pray, "Let the anointing of the Spirit fall on me," and we sing about wanting the Spirit's anointing so we can be more connected with God, more filled with His power. We give the impression that this anointing is something "out there" somewhere that we want to come over us.

But the way I see it, we need to come up with a different word for that, because the Bible says we already have the Spirit's anointing. It's already within us. The apostle John says to all believers, "You have been anointed by the Holy One" (1 John 2:20). A bit later he adds, "The anointing that you received from him abides in you, and you have no need that anyone should teach you" (v. 27).

This anointing from the Spirit is like a satellite dish deep inside us. It's the receiver for invisible divine signals, so we're able to pick up every communication God wants to send our way, even though we can't see Him.

And because He's a person, your experience of divine power and divine communication is fully dependent upon your personal relationship with Him. The better you know Him, the more you'll experience everything He is and everything He has for you.

The way to experience His power is not by going power hunting...but by going person hunting. The more you pursue and relate to this person, the more He will amaze you with all that He has to offer.

Chapter 3

THE ACTIVATION

So you're thinking, *Yes, I want this! I want a closer relationship with the Holy Spirit so I can experience more of His supernatural presence and see my life changed. How do I make it happen?*

STARTING THE ENGINE

When you buy an automobile, it comes with an indwelling power. It's called an engine, and it lives under the hood inside the car. This engine is the force designed to transport you in your car at a remarkable rate of speed to wherever you choose to drive it.

However, as you sit behind the wheel in your new car with that indwelt engine, just wanting to drive away is not enough to make it happen. To get the car moving out of the parking lot and onto the highway, the engine must first be

---

The Holy Spirit is

God's engine

indwelling you.

So how do you

turn the key?

—— ⚚ ——

---

engaged—it must be ignited. And that requires an act of your will: You have to turn the ignition key.

The Holy Spirit is God's engine indwelling you. So how do you turn the key? What act of your will does it take to start the engine—so the Holy Spirit doesn't simply lie dormant within you, but you can move forward by His energy onto the highway of life toward successful, victorious, empowered Christian living?

WHERE IT BEGINS

Living by the Spirit's power begins in your thinking. That's where the ignition happens.

Notice closely how Paul explains it:

> For those who live according to the flesh *set their minds* on the things of the flesh, but those who live according to the Spirit *set their minds* on the things of the Spirit. To *set the mind* on the flesh is death, but to *set the mind* on the Spirit is life and peace. (Romans 8:5–6)

To live according to the Spirit means first of all to think in alignment with what the Spirit is thinking.

It's to think in terms of what *God* says about everything, not what you're saying or thinking yourself or what anybody else says about you. "Let God be true, and every man a liar," Paul wrote (Romans 3:4, NIV), and every human being lies at times, including yourself. God wants us to turn away from human misconceptions and deceptions and delusions, and instead accept as accurate what *He* says about us.

Two Radio Stations

Your mind is like a radio that picks up two stations. One of them is the Fleshly Broadcast Network, FBN. You've always been able to pick up that station; in fact, for a while it was the only signal you received.

The other station is the Heavenly Broadcast Network, HBN, which you've only been able to tune in to since the Holy Spirit came to live inside you and transformed your reception capability.

So now you have a choice. You can determine which station you listen to. Both are always on the air, pouring out a constant stream of programming. The entertainment and information on FBN is constantly pumping and promoting and amusing your flesh. The music and the talk often sound true and feel true, but everything on FBN is laced with lies, and it drags you down.

Meanwhile, everything on HBN is truth for your soul.

It lifts you higher and inspires you upward to attain all the freedom and adventure that you were truly created for.

The listening choice is yours.

RATS ON BOARD

In the early days of aviation, Frederick Handley Page of England was one of the pioneers. The story is told of how he once was flying alone in one of the early small planes when he detected a disturbing sound behind him in the cargo area. He soon realized it was a rat, gnawing on the plane's control cables—a disaster in the making.

This was in the days before autopilot, so he couldn't just leave the controls and go back and kill the rat. But what could he do?

Then he remembered that if he could gain sufficient altitude, the decrease in oxygen would be fatal for the rat. At once he flew the plane higher…then higher…and eventually he no longer heard that gnawing sound. Later, after safely landing, he found the rat's dead body.

Maybe you feel as if there's something gnawing at your life, trying to bring you down and destroy you. If you've got rats on board, the first step to knocking them lifeless is to take your thinking upward to new heights—to "set your minds on things that are above" (Colossians 3:2).

GETTING USED TO A NEW NAME

To think higher, are you staying actively aware of the fact that the real you is your new, Spirit-given identity in Christ, not your old identity in Adam?

This new identity is so basic that we've even received a new name—Christian—for we've been newly adopted into Christ's family.

Sometimes new names require a little getting used to. A week after my wife and I were married, we traveled to New York to be involved in a ministry, and we were staying in a church. One day my wife answered the church's phone, and the caller asked, "Can I talk to Mrs. Evans please?" My wife asked the person to hold the line, and then went to find someone there by that name. Half a minute later, it dawned on her: *She* was Mrs. Evans.

She came back to the phone, altered her voice, and said, "Yes?"

So many times we as Christians forget who we are. We've grown so accustomed to our old name, our old life, our old ways of thinking and talking and relating that we forget the newness that is ours to embrace. Being forgetful like that doesn't mean we'll get evicted from God's family; it just means our relationship with the Lord needs revitalizing. Our mental focus needs sharpening.

GOD'S WITNESS PROTECTION PROGRAM

Our new Spirit-given identity is so potent that it provides us with overwhelming spiritual protection, and God's Word gives us the reason: "He who is in you is greater than he who is in the world" (1 John 4:4).

Some decades ago, to help fight organized crime, federal law enforcement developed a witness protection program to help guard the lives of informants. The program relocates these people and gives them new social security numbers, new driver's license numbers, new bank accounts, and much more— all to shield them from their enemies still lurking in the crime world. The Holy Spirit's baptism is like that. Because of our new name and new identity our enemy no longer has any final claim over us. We're in God's witness protection program.

> You don't have to wait to go to heaven to be in heaven.

And though we're still in the world, yet in a real sense we've also been relocated. Our new residence is situated in "the heavenly realms," according to what Paul tells us in Ephesians. We're actually up there already: "God raised us up with Christ and seated us with him in the heavenly realms in Christ Jesus" (Ephesians 2:6, NIV). Our transfer has already transpired; our move has been made. In a spiritually genuine sense, you don't have to wait to *go* to heaven to *be* in heaven; God has placed us there already with Christ.

ACTUAL HEAVEN

Maybe you've tried one of those virtual reality experiences—where they set you up with special headgear and goggles, and without going anywhere you're off to some real-looking realm in computer zoo-zoo land. The Holy Spirit does better than that—with the Spirit, you're actually there in heavenly places, seated next to Jesus Christ. It's Actual Reality, the real thing.

Of course, the place where you physically walk and breathe and eat and sleep is earth, not heaven. But you can find a piece of heaven on earth, particularly in the church—since the Spirit's baptism always fuses believers together in this new environment. The Holy Spirit's job is to make God's presence evident and perceptible in this world, and He does that most noticeably through the church.

Christ's church on earth is like an embassy in a foreign land. In our nation's capital, you can go to the Turkish embassy or the Kenyan embassy or the Irish embassy and experience a little piece of Turkey or Kenya or Ireland right in this country, a specific piece of ground that these other nations are sovereign over. Likewise, the true church is where God is fully sovereign and present to pour out His blessing in the midst of this world—a world that, for a little while longer, is still the enemy's domain.

In a unique way, a little piece of heaven is inside you as well, since God's presence actually lives in you through the Spirit. *God* inside you equals *heaven* inside you. That's another way of saying you already possess eternal life and can never lose it.

WORM FOOD

Going higher in our thinking also means we have to recognize God's perspective on our flesh—our natural self. And God's perspective about our flesh is that it's totally unfixable.

Most Christians try to have victory over the flesh by getting their flesh to do better. But that's impossible—sin's power can never be whipped by human effort, because our flesh cannot be reformed. Paul knew this firsthand: "I know that nothing good dwells in me, that is, in my flesh" (Romans 7:18). Nothing we do can make our flesh less prone to sin.

> Sin's power can never be whipped by human effort, because our flesh cannot be reformed.

Our flesh is ultimately good for only one thing, and that's worm food. God isn't even in the business of trying to fix our flesh; instead, He's planning to give us a whole new body in eternity because the one we currently have is wrecked beyond repair.

Meanwhile, however, we're stuck in these shells. And that causes problems.

Paul lays out the situation in Romans 7: "I do not understand my own actions," he says. "For I do not do what I want, but I do the very thing I hate" (v. 15). Can you relate to that? "I have the desire to do what is right," Paul confesses, "but not the ability to carry it out. For I do not do the good I want, but the evil I do not want is what I keep on doing" (vv. 18–19).

Paul feels like a prisoner—he says he's "captive to the law of sin" (v. 23). Then he cries out, "Wretched man that I am! Who will deliver me from this body of death?" (v. 24).

DRAGGING THE CORPSE

Those words bring to mind a form of capital punishment that was sometimes carried out in those days. They would take a dead body and strap it to you; everywhere you went, you had to drag the corpse along as well. You can imagine how strong a desire you would have to get free of it. That was the longing Paul had as he realized the wretchedness of his natural flesh and asked for deliverance. Who would deliver him from that "body of death"?

Sometimes we cry out for the same thing. We want freedom, we want spiritual power, but our flesh is trained and programmed and so efficient at doing wrong. We've tried encounter groups, we've made our New Year's resolutions, we've read the surefire advice in articles and books, but we still keep dragging around the old life with its passions. We try hard, then we try still harder—but hateful attitudes and wasteful habits and insensitive speech and simmering lusts keep pulling us down. Self-improvement just doesn't cut it.

So who will deliver us?

GRAVITY OVERRULED

There *is* deliverance, and Paul knows it—so he's able to shout at the end of Romans 7, "Thanks be to God through Jesus Christ our Lord!" (v. 25).

Then he explains (in Romans 8) how the deliverance comes—it's through the Holy Spirit. Paul says there's a higher law that sets us free from the deadly and burdensome law of sin: "For the law of the Spirit of life has set you free in Christ Jesus from the law of sin and death" (v. 2).

You learned long ago that there's a law that keeps things down on the ground instead of flying off into the sky. It's called the law of gravity.

But airplanes don't obey that law. Why not?

It's not that gravity doesn't exist for airplanes, but that the law of gravity is transcended by something else, the laws of aerodynamics. When you take an object of a particular design and apply a certain power thrust, a certain speed, you get a certain lift.

Airplanes don't negate the law of gravity; they just override it with a higher law.

So it is with your life and mine. When the Spirit takes over, He doesn't cancel the deadly law of sin in our lives—sin still tries to do its thing to us—but the Spirit overrules and supersedes the law of sin with *a new law,* a higher law—the law of the Spirit that gives life, enabling us to soar.

INSIDE OUT

That higher law is also a deeper law, the deepest thing about you. The spiritual life must be lived and nourished from the inside out, but most of us try to do it from the outside in; we think the way to get spiritual benefit, or the way to fix anything that might be wrong inside us, is to do enough of the right external stuff. But that's all backwards, and here's why.

In every person who hasn't come to faith in Christ, the spirit is dead—there's no life principle inside their spirit. It's as if they did not even have a spirit. The most important thing about their God-designed humanity is missing. It's a

> The Spirit overrules the law of sin with a new law, a higher law.

deficiency and a deformity so severe that it results in confusion and scarring to their mind and emotions, which in turn negatively impacts their physical well-being and behavior.

But once you come to Christ and receive God's gift of the Holy Spirit within you, your spirit is converted, redeemed, made alive. In a new Spirit-to-spirit connection, the Holy Spirit's job is now to control and influence and enliven everything about you, *starting from the inside out.* A reforming and transforming process is triggered that will work itself out from your spirit, breaking through to your mind and emotions and will, then flowing outward into your body, so you can live a brand-new life in public.

But it must be activated from the inside out.

It's a lot like popping popcorn. In each kernel of corn there is moisture. When popcorn is placed in the microwave, the energy and heat of the radiation turns that moisture into steam. The steam expands and presses against the external shell until the pressure's so great that the seed pops—and becomes transformed. What was contained internally is now expressed on the outside; the hard external gives way to the soft, eatable inside. And what's amazing about this process is that you would have never known by looking that the external shell had so much on the inside.

Likewise, when the fire of the Holy Spirit is ignited in a believer's life, the Spirit transforms the soul (personality), and the transformed soul changes the behavior of the body. The new life on the inside becomes the dominant expression of the visible life on the outside. The Holy Spirit wants to renovate us from the inside out—"spirit and soul and body" (1 Thessalonians 5:23).

Chapter 4

UNDER THE INFLUENCE

To know the Spirit better and experience more of His vitality, and to be transformed from the inside out, what else do we need to know?

To help us capture what life in the Spirit is all about, the Scriptures give us two strong images to ponder—being *filled* with the Spirit and *walking* in the Spirit. Both are profound and powerful in their simplicity. Let's look first at the Spirit's filling.

BEING FILLED

The baptism of the Spirit and the indwelling of the Spirit are automatic with your conversion. There's no command in the Bible for believers to become Spirit-baptized or to become Spirit-indwelt, because the Spirit has already baptized believers and already indwells believers.

But we do have this command in the Bible: "Be filled with the Spirit" (Ephesians 5:18).

It's a command that comes immediately after Paul tells the Ephesians to wake up from sleep, to walk wisely, to make good use of their time, and to not be foolish. You see, you can be a Christian and be asleep and unaware, you can be a Christian and waste time, you can be a Christian and be unwise and foolish. You can make those mistakes even as a believer, or else Paul wouldn't need to tell them not to make them.

So the question is, what's the most important thing I can do so that I'm an alive Christian, not a sleeper Christian? So that I'm a time investor, not a time waster? So that I'm wise and not foolish?

You can't change those things just because you want to change. You must be filled with the Spirit—so that He's fully flowing, fully functioning, in full control within you.

A Word to All Churches

When we in the church fail to experience deliverance and empowerment and transformation, the problem for most of us isn't a lack of Bible teaching. We have church services, we have Christian radio and television, we have Christian books. We have Christian counseling and seminars and workshops and programs and ministries. We aren't lacking in those areas.

What we're lacking in our churches is the filling of the Holy Spirit.

In fact, let me make this bold statement to every local church: The fuller of the Spirit you are, the fewer "programs" you need. Because no program on earth can match the filling from heaven. Counseling would be cut short if more people who are being counseled were instead being filled.

The church's job is not to replace the filling of the Spirit. The Bible tells us we're not to neglect meeting together, and we have a responsibility to be orderly and organized as we do that. But we must never let organization or programs replace the Spirit's filling. Our institutional efforts, no matter how hard we try, will never be able to do what the Holy Spirit can do when the church is obediently filled with God's Holy Spirit.

Why aren't more of our churches experiencing the supernatural? Because they're not Spirit-

> The church's job is not to replace the filling of the Spirit.

filled churches. They may be Bible-teaching churches—and thank God for that. They may have great programs and great facilities. But unless the Spirit is filling them, the supernatural will not be seen. Where there is no filling, there is no wind and fire from heaven.

LET HIM FILL YOU

What does it mean to "be filled with the Spirit"?

Let's make a few fundamental observations about that verse in Ephesians 5.

One, it's a command, not a suggestion. "Be filled." God is not asking you; He's telling you. And your obedient response must involve an act of your will.

Two, it's passive. The Spirit does the filling—our job is to let Him do it. That means we can't already be full of ourselves. We have to empty ourselves of pride and presumption and self-dependence. That's something we're usually not very good at; we try, but we're like a plastic milk jug after the last glass of milk has been poured from it—the jug isn't really clean inside; there's still a residue there. And to remove it we need to fill that jug clear to the top with fresh, cleansing water, just as the Holy Spirit fills us up to clean us out.

Three, the command in Ephesians 5:18 is plural—it applies to everyone. It's for all Christians, not just some spiritually elite group. Every believer is to be filled with the Spirit.

And four, this command is in the present tense; it's continuous. We're to *keep on* being filled. You can't get filled yesterday and expect it to last for today. Filling today doesn't mean filling tomorrow.

FRESH FILL-UPS

We regularly take our cars to a filling station. Why? So we can fill them with fuel. Why? So we can go where we want to go.

And after you drive up to that filling station, they don't give you a new motor. No, your indwelling motor is there to stay inside your car. But unless that motor gets fuel, you're going nowhere. So you fill 'er up.

However, the very second you pull away from that filling station and head to the highway, the fuel begins dissipating. You're burning it up, consuming it. You begin to lose the filling. The farther you go and the faster you go, the less fuel you have, and so you have to get filled up again.

It's the same way with the Spirit. We constantly need fresh wind, fresh fire, to enable us to live out God's expectations for us in this world, to empower us each day to go where He wants us go and do what He wants us to do.

LIKE DRUNKENNESS

Paul makes a point of comparing the Spirit's filling with being drunk with wine. He says, "And do not get drunk with wine, for that is debauchery, but be filled with the Spirit" (v. 18).

Being drunk means to be controlled by alcohol; you do things you don't naturally do, you act in ways you don't naturally act.

Being Spirit-filled means to be controlled by the Spirit, to be under the influence of the Spirit. He dominates your personality; He runs the show and calls the shots. He dictates your actions and reactions.

BREAKING US FIRST

In order to dominate us like that, the Holy Spirit must break us. He must shatter our self-sufficiency, our independence.

One of the main ways He does this is through trials. He puts us in situations to tear down our assumption that we can fix ourselves on our own. Through trials He wants to bring us to the point of surrender (1 Peter 4:1–2).

To dominate us, the Holy Spirit must break us.

He's like a wrangler breaking a wild horse. The stallion prefers to do his own thing, and when the wrangler hops on his back, that horse bucks and rears and does everything he can to shake that rider for good. He's thinking, *I won't have anybody controlling me, telling me what to do, running my life. Get off my back!*

But no matter how many times the rider gets thrown, he hops back on and keeps riding, until that worn-out creature beneath him gets his point: "Your old life is over, Buster, and I'm in charge now." The horse yields at last to the rider's control. He hasn't lost his identity or his physical strength—but that identity and strength are now under the control of another.

BE A GUZZLER

When you're under the Spirit's control, He enables you to do what *He* naturally does instead of what you naturally do. You care for people you would naturally ignore. You're patient when you would normally lose your temper. You have peace when you would usually be in turmoil. Hate gives way to love, stubbornness to understanding, dissension to unity. All unnatural! And all because you're "drunk" with the Spirit.

Now there's only one way I know of to get drunk. And that's to drink.

A drunk man didn't get drunk by wishing and hoping for alcohol, or talking about alcohol, or staring at alcohol. He gets drunk only by drinking. And we're to do the same with the Holy Spirit.

Some of us are only sippers instead of drinkers. To drink full is to do what Jesus taught when He told us to let His words abide in us (John 15:7). We let the flow of His life enter our lives and surge there. We let His words dominate us, and we find ability we didn't know we had; we discover a power we didn't know existed; we experience a personality change we didn't think possible.

So when it comes to the Spirit, don't just sip. Start drinking deep; start guzzling!

THE WORSHIP THAT FILLS

How do we do that? How do we drink the Spirit and let Him fill us?

After giving the command to be Spirit-filled, Paul goes on to explain and illustrate it for us. He shows us that more than anything else, it's worship that fills you with the Spirit. Look at what he says:

> Be filled with the Spirit, addressing one another in psalms and hymns and spiritual songs, singing and making melody to the Lord with all your heart, giving thanks always and for everything to God the Father in the name of our Lord Jesus Christ, submitting to one another out of reverence for Christ. (Ephesians 5:18–21)

What does all that mean? Fundamentally it means making worship a lifestyle, not just a once-a-week event or a five-minute fix every morning or evening.

For our devotions, many of us faithfully follow the rule: A verse a day keeps the devil away. We add a few quick words of prayer, then we're off to take care of pressing business. But that isn't drinking deep. That isn't abiding. That isn't worship as a lifestyle.

Lifestyle worship means the daily domination of God in your life. It means continual awareness of God's worth and of our absolute dependence on Him by making our decisions in accordance with His Word. It means expressing joy and trust and gratefulness in your relationship with God. And it means serving the Lord in a way that overflows into continual service to those around you.

So if you want to be a Spirit-filled individual, you must be a worshiping individual. If we want a Spirit-filled family, we must be a worshiping family. If we want a Spirit-filled church, we must be a worshiping church.

If we want to see God's supernatural fire fall upon us and ignite our lives, if we want to feel His supernatural wind blow upon us and stir us to holiness, then let us worship God the Father and the Lord Jesus Christ, and let us worship in spirit and in truth.

Chapter 5

FORWARD, STEP-BY-STEP

Along with being filled, a second profound analogy in Scripture of living by the Spirit is simply that of walking. "If we live by the Spirit," Paul says, "let us also walk by the Spirit" (Galatians 5:25).

Now this simple image has some important implications.

If you're walking, it usually means you're going somewhere. You have a destination. And your destination as you walk in the Spirit is to live for the will of God. In your relationships and activities at home and at work and wherever you are, you're telling your Father, "I want to do what pleases You." The Holy Spirit's destination for us is holiness and conformity to the image of Christ.

Walking also implies continuous motion, sustained forward progress. One step after another after another.

And it's active, not passive. It's not sitting back and relaxing and letting up and letting go. Walking in the Spirit doesn't mean the Spirit does everything while you do nothing.

Walking is measured and balanced in its pace. It's not the same as huff-and-puff running. It's not roaring ahead at burnout speed. It's a step-by-step approach to life, taking each thing as it comes on the path the Spirit leads us on, consciously bringing the Spirit of God to bear—by prayerful obedience to God's Word—in every situation, every circumstance.

Finally, and most important, to walk "in the Spirit" implies that this is a dependent kind of walking, since the weight of the entire body is carried by the alternating movements of the legs. The act of walking sounds simple enough, but we need help to do it in the way God intends.

A LIVING, LOVING CRUTCH

A month after I got married, I got hit with a cross-body block on a football field. My cleat failed to come out of the mud, and my leg snapped in half. My tibia and fibula were shattered, and I was taken by ambulance to a hospital where they cut open my leg and set the bones, then put me in a sixty-pound hip-to-foot cast. The break took six months to heal—six months of walking on a pair of wooden crutches.

Those crutches were strong, and with them I could do what I otherwise couldn't—I could walk. I could get around. I dared not take a step without them, lest I fall and reinjure my leg. I wouldn't have made it back then without those crutches.

But I had another crutch, too, one that I liked better than the wooden ones. Sometimes the wooden ones were out of reach, so I put my arm around my wife's shoulder, and she put her arm around my waist. Yes, I liked that living crutch much better, because those wooden crutches didn't care for me and love me like she did.

That's what the Holy Spirit is. He's a living crutch who loves you, a crutch who cares for you. And if you'll depend on Him by prayerful obedience to God's Word, you'll find that He's plenty strong enough to hold all your weight and all your burdens, yet sensitive enough to whisper in your ear, telling you where to go and what to do and how to do it in accordance with His revealed will. He's wise enough to take you by the best path to your destination, and compassionate enough to encourage you all the way there.

THE PROOF OF DEPENDENCE

So walking in the Spirit is a dependent kind of walking. The Holy Spirit stands beside us, ready to deliver whatever kind of support we may require in order to successfully live for Christ.

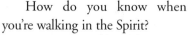

> Prayer is the
> proof of
> dependence on
> the Spirit.

How do you know when you're walking in the Spirit?

You know it when you're living a life of prayer, because prayer is the proof of dependence on the Spirit.

Paul says we should be "praying at all times in the Spirit, with all prayer and supplication" (Ephesians 6:18). With each step you take in daily life, you pray—silently or aloud. *Lord, in this responsibility facing me now, I'm counting on You to help me be my best and do my best. I ask You, Lord, to give me sensitivity and understanding in this conflict with my wife. Lord, grant me wisdom in carrying out this discipline of my child. Holy Spirit, open the eyes of my heart as I look to God's Word to speak to me.*

You're not ashamed to pray again and again, *Help me…. Help me…. Help me….*

GROANINGS

Especially in prayer we discover that "the Spirit helps us in our weakness. For we do not know what to pray for as we ought, but the Spirit himself intercedes for us with groanings too deep for words" (Romans 8:26). What better prayer partner could we ask for than the Holy Spirit Himself?

Experiencing that help sometimes leads to groaning.

Your heart's desire is to do God's will in the decisions and circumstances and trials you face, but sometimes you're confused and troubled, and your problems seem to be getting worse, not better. And so, not knowing how to pray, you groan.

It's like the groaning of a mother in the labor of childbirth. She's in agony because of the pain, but it's agony with a purpose. With her every contraction and her every groan, the baby within her is saying, "Let me out of here!" The more groaning, the closer the birth.

The more you groan like this in your prayers in the Spirit (which is praying in accordance with God's Word and His will), the closer you're coming to God, the closer you are to seeing His answers and His blessing in your circumstances.

The groans of the Spirit are good groans. We can trust that the Spirit knows what He's doing because the next verse tells us "The Spirit intercedes for the saints according to the will of God" (v. 27). And the next verse after that gives us confidence that our groaning is purposeful and effective: "And we know that for those who love God all things work together for good" (v. 28).

So don't feel bad if things get worse when you are praying and groaning to God; it just means something good is coming down the birth canal!

BORROWING FROM GOD

As you grow into this walk of dependence through the Holy Spirit's control and influence, then where you once said, "I just can't do it," you now say, "I can do all things through Him who strengthens me" (Philippians 4:13).

That's because walking in God's Spirit means that you are in fact borrowing from God's power (1 Peter 1:3).

If you could give me the mind Einstein had, there's no mathematical formula I could not unravel. If you give me the fingers of Mozart, there's no tune I couldn't play. Give me Michael Jordan's legs and Hank Aaron's arms, and there's no sports contest in which I couldn't excel.

> Walking in God's Spirit means you are in fact borrowing from God's power.

And if you give me the life of Jesus Christ…there's no spiritual victory I cannot achieve!

Paul says, "I have been crucified with Christ. It is no longer I who live, but Christ who lives in me" (Galatians 2:20). Paul had no qualms in saying, "I borrow from God—I can't live the Christian life on my own, so I had to die to my own human efforts."

Most Christians don't believe that. Most Christians believe they can pull off most of the Christian life, until they get to the "biggies"; only then do they need God.

But that's opposite of Paul's thinking. Paul speaks freely about "the help of the Spirit of Jesus Christ" in dealing with life's circumstances (Philippians 1:19). That's the same help that we desperately need in every arena of life, and the same help that the Spirit freely offers you and me.

EASY STRIDES

One day I was dashing through an airport terminal, trying to catch a plane that I was in danger of missing.

As I hurried along, I suddenly began to notice something. Though I relaxed my pace to an easier stride, I was smoothly and quickly passing people on both sides of me along the corridor. It was almost as if I were flying through that airport.

Where did all this power come from to enable me to outpace the other people with no more effort than if I were only casually strolling along? What was the source of this amazing capacity?

I'll tell you: It was the moving sidewalk I stepped onto. My strides were now applied on top of another power. Underneath me was a force taking me farther and faster, yet with less exertion. I had a heightened capability to get where I needed to go. I was still stepping forward, but my effort was fueled by a power greater than my own.

That's what walking in dependence on the Spirit is like.

Chapter 6

THE CRITICAL BLOW
IN THE BATTLE

Maybe you're now thinking, *Okay, I understand all you're saying—about the need to be filled with and dependent on the Spirit, and the need to pray, and especially the need to think the right thoughts. But I've tried that approach when I want to stop sinning, and it isn't working. When the flesh entices, I tell myself I really don't have to yield to that temptation, but the feelings just grow stronger—my flesh fights harder, and it usually wins.*

Most of us at that point surrender to the flesh instead of going on to strike the critical blow, using our most important weapon in the battle. Let's take a closer look at it.

THE SPARKS FLY

First of all, how clearly do you understand the serious nature and extent of this battle—this war that's raging inside you?

Maybe you know a man and a woman who live under the same roof as husband and wife, and yet they can't seem to get along. They have differing perspectives on things, separate ambitions, divergent attitudes, clashing outlooks.

> How clearly do you understand this war that's raging inside you?

So the tension in their house is constant, and the sparks often fly.

That's what it's like with the Spirit and your flesh. Both dwell in the same house (your body), but they can't stand each other, so there's unceasing warfare between them. The flesh has its purposes and sharpens its weapons to fight the Spirit. The Spirit has His purposes and takes aim against the flesh.

Paul makes the conflict clear: "For the desires of the flesh are *against* the Spirit, and the desires of the Spirit are *against* the flesh, for these are *opposed* to each other, to keep you from doing the things you want to do" (Galatians 5:17).

You know what it's like: You want to follow Christ, and by the Spirit's leading you're ready to do just that. But your flesh is like the defensive line of an opposing football team, lined up against you, determined to block your forward progress. The Holy Spirit has to lead you forward like a pulling offensive guard, crashing that defensive line to break open your path, allowing you to sprint to the goal line.

ACTIVE RESISTANCE

Every time your flesh seeks to gain control of your actions, the Spirit will actively oppose it. That's why sometimes when you're on the verge of doing something wrong, the phone will ring or something else will happen to redirect your attention and help you choose the particular "way of escape" that God always offers whenever you face temptation (1 Corinthians 10:13). And even when you fail to take the way of escape, the Holy Spirit will be actively at work to make sure you don't feel good about it. A Christian is capable of committing any sin a non-Christian commits— a Christian just can't do it without tension and conflict, and without initially feeling guilt as a result.

Meanwhile, the flesh is just as active in resisting the Spirit. That's why after you have an encounter with God in His Word or in prayer or in worship, and you feel yourself rising to a spiritual high, suddenly you find yourself getting ticked off at something somebody says to you. Or your flesh will resurrect some disgusting thought or shameful memory that you buried long ago.

What your flesh still wants to do above all else is to hinder or stifle or stunt your spiritual progress. It wants to keep you from experiencing the life of God in your day-to-day living and make you a hostage to your old patterns of living. For example, as you face difficulties and obstacles in life, your flesh will get you to look for solutions you can control yourself, such as changing jobs, changing mates, or changing locations, instead of having you engage your new identity in Christ and depend on the Holy Spirit's guidance through every challenge. Your flesh will want you to feel trapped by its desires, so you relate more with those cravings than you do with your new identity in Christ.

THE POWER TO SAY NO

But the bold promise of Scripture is this: "Walk by the Spirit, and you will not gratify the desires of the flesh" (Galatians 5:16).

Now don't misread that verse. It doesn't say that if you walk by the Spirit you will not *have* the desires of the flesh—but only that you won't gratify them, that you won't fulfill them.

Sometimes we think, *If I was really a spiritual Christian, I wouldn't even want to do this sin.* But don't get upset and frustrated because your flesh keeps wanting to do what's wrong; that's simply what the flesh does by nature, and always will. And the flesh is extremely experienced and proficient at it. So your flesh keeps telling you, "You've got to have it!" (whatever "it" is for you at that moment), and that's exactly how you often feel: You've got to have it *now!*

Although God's Holy Spirit doesn't automatically suppress the flesh's desires, His promise is that even now you'll have the full power to say no to them. You can tell your flesh what to do instead of the flesh telling you what to do.

> Don't get frustrated because your flesh keeps wanting to do what's wrong.

It's also important to read the order of this promise. You don't try to put the flesh to death so you can walk in the Spirit; rather, you walk in the Spirit, which gives you power and victory over the desires of the flesh.

THE CRITICAL BLOW

If you rely only on your feelings as you enter the next round in this continuing fight between your flesh and the Spirit, be assured that the flesh will win.

But if you want to strike the critical blow in fighting the flesh, then fully engage your mind in an active response that relies on the Spirit…and then actually step out in faith by acting in accordance with God's Word.

You pray something like this:

"Lord God, I don't have the ability to pull off what I truly want to do right now in obedience to You. I can think about the right reaction, I can see it in my mind; but that's not my problem. My problem is *stepping* it. My problem is walking it. My problem is living it out.

"You tell me that I don't have to indulge in what my flesh is craving. You tell me I don't have to go there. You tell me I have a new identity in Christ and that my deepest desire is actually to turn to You and find the help I need. I believe You're telling me the truth about that.

"And because I believe You, I'm, therefore, going to take this step of obedience and move away from what my lying flesh is pressuring me to do.

"And since I don't have the power on my own to keep walking in the right direction You've pointed out to me, I'm now banking on Your Holy Spirit to give me the ability to accomplish it. The Holy Spirit is Your gift to me to help me live out the obedience and the victory You've created me for. So I embrace the gift of the Holy Spirit. And I'm stepping out—in faith, based on Your Word."

Do that, and you'll discover the ability to keep taking steps into a level of victory that you could not even imagine before. The cravings of the flesh will rear their ugly heads again, but those feelings will lose their controlling edge. By the Spirit's promise and presence, you will not carry out the desires of your flesh.

YOUR RESPONSIBILITY

Can you see how the Spirit's power and your own responsibility work together?

Paul puts it this way:

> For if you live according to the flesh you will die,
> but if by the Spirit you put to death the deeds of
> the body, you will live. (Romans 8:13)

Though you do this "by the Spirit," it's *you* who must do it.

You must do it—but it's by means of the power of another person—the Holy Spirit of God. You make the choice, and you carry it out by resting upon and drawing upon a power beyond your own. You actively count on the Holy Spirit to give you the ability to do what He wants you to do.

This isn't simply the power of positive thinking; in fact, it's the opposite of that—and infinitely greater. The positive thinking approach tells us to just say no to a sin and to convince ourselves that we'll conquer it— "I believe it, I commit to it, I can and will do it." But that's still human power. The Christian says, "I know I can't do it on my own. It's only by the Holy Spirit's power within me."

You'll discover a level of victory you could not even imagine before.

Chapter 7

EVER-FLOWING FREEDOM

When I was a boy growing up in Baltimore, the fire marshal would sometimes come around on a hot summer afternoon and flush out one of the fire hydrants. Water would surge up out of the hydrant and come splashing down on the street, and all of us kids would put on short pants and run through it. That was our inner-city swimming pool.

But it posed a problem in my mind. I couldn't figure out how that three-foot-high hydrant could produce so much water, hour after hour.

I decided to ask my dad: "Dad, how can that little pipe hold all that water?"

He smiled and said, "Son, that pipe is empty." Then he explained that the hydrant was joined underground with other pipes that were connected to a reservoir—a lake that held more water than I could imagine, more than we could all use even on the hottest summer afternoon. The rush of water from the hydrant was made possible by that hidden connection to a boundless, unseen source of water.

We're like that empty hydrant pipe; we hold nothing in ourselves, but the Holy Spirit is our invisible connection to almighty God, who has an infinite reservoir of refreshment that never runs dry. Because of that connection, you can open up your life to Him at any time and experience the living waters flowing up from your innermost being, meeting your every need.

THE THIRST QUENCHER

When you think about it, one of the most thrilling New Testament pictures of the Spirit's work is this one in John's Gospel:

> Jesus stood up and cried out, "If anyone thirsts, let him come to me and drink. Whoever believes in me, as the Scripture has said, 'Out of his heart will flow rivers of living water'" (John 7:37–38).

John immediately adds this explanation: "Now this he said about the Spirit" (v. 39).

The Spirit is like an indwelling pump that gushes forth the thirst-quenching waters of the spiritual, supernatural life in an unlimited supply.

I think that's why God's Holy Spirit takes on many names in Scripture. Besides being our "Counselor" or "Helper," He's also "the Spirit of truth," "the Spirit of holiness," "the Spirit of life," "the Spirit of adoption as sons," "the Spirit of wisdom," and "the Spirit of grace" (John 15:26; 14:17; Romans 1:4; 8:2; 8:15; Ephesians 1:17, NIV; Hebrews 10:29). In other words, as He fills you, *He will be to you whatever you need.*

In this ever-flowing fullness, the Spirit will always be there to liberate us from anything that would enslave us. When we come to Christ and receive His Holy Spirit, we also receive—for the first time in our lives—the capacity to be truly free. "Where the Spirit of the Lord is, there is freedom" (2 Corinthians 3:17).

> As He fills you, He will be to you whatever you need.

You may be in bondage even now to a way of thinking you can't shake or to habits you can't break. But the Lord's promise in the Spirit is for your full and lasting freedom.

KNOW AND ENJOY YOUR FREEDOM

In Texas where I live, our holiday known as Juneteenth had its origins in the Civil War. President Lincoln's Emancipation Proclamation had granted freedom—as of

January 1, 1863—to the slaves in all states still at war with the Union. That included Texas, but most Texas slaves weren't aware of this until the war's end more than two years later. On June 19, 1865, a major general in the U.S. Army issued a proclamation in Galveston declaring that slaves in Texas indeed had been given their liberty. After that, June 19 became a day of celebration each year, and now it's even a Texas state holiday.

For two years, African-Americans in Texas had continued in bondage, living like slaves and thinking like slaves, when in fact—in the eyes of the nation and the world—they were free. Likewise in the spiritual realm, some of us are living and thinking like slaves when we don't have to be, because we haven't understood that we've actually been set free. We're still controlled by masters who have no legitimate ownership over us.

Jesus said, "The Spirit of the Lord...has sent me to proclaim liberty to the captives" (Luke 4:18). He also said, "If the Son sets you free, you will be free indeed" (John 8:36). You can fully enjoy this freedom as you let the Spirit dominate your thinking, as you yield your life to His control. Then you'll know you're free indeed.

THE FREEDOM THAT'S A LIE

This freedom never means simply doing whatever your flesh wants, because that kind of "freedom" is a lie. Suppose a fish said, "I'm tired of being in the water all the time, and I want out. I want to be free to run along the hills with the horses and scurry up trees like the squirrel and slide through the grass like a snake." That fish isn't asking for freedom; he's asking for death.

God's will and design for us is like water to a fish—our only real freedom is to be inside it; outside of it there's only death. The freedom the Spirit brings us is a positive freedom—the actual ability and capacity to be all God wants us to be and to do all that He wants us to do.

> Our only real freedom is to be inside God's will; outside of it there's only death.

FREE FROM INSECURITY

The Spirit liberates us first of all from any uncertainty about our salvation. He secures our relationship with God eternally, and He lets us know it: "The Spirit himself bears witness with our spirit that we are children of God" (Romans 8:16).

If you're truly saved, you can never lose your salvation. Now that's good news—God loves you enough to keep you! Having believed in Christ, "you were marked in him with a seal, the promised Holy Spirit, who is a deposit guaranteeing our inheritance" (Ephesians 1:13–14, NIV).

So you're sealed, and to break that seal and become unsaved you would have to be more powerful than the seal, which means more powerful than the One who set the seal, and that's God Himself. Therefore it's impossible to break.

The security of the believer is one of the great doctrines of the Bible, but it poses great problems for some. I understand their fears. They worry that if someone thinks he can never lose his salvation, he'll just go out and sin all he wants to, with no sense of responsibility and no fear of God.

But that's like someone having a health insurance policy and then deciding, "Now that treatment regarding my health is secured, I can go jump off skyscrapers and drive my car over cliffs all I want to." You would know that person just doesn't understand his insurance policy. The policy isn't there to let you act like a fool; it's there to let you know you're covered if you get in trouble. And that makes you grateful for it.

It's only when we don't understand our salvation that we abuse it. When you truly appreciate the grace of God and the stability of our salvation by the blood of Christ, we react with gratitude, not abuse.

His security is like the cocoon around a butterfly. In this life, you're encased firmly in God's love and grace while you undergo an amazing metamorphosis, until someday you break forth at last in perfect form to fly with bright color and beauty and glory. You were an ugly caterpillar before, slimy and slow, but never again. What is on the inside is seeking to break forth to manifest the new, true you that God has created.

FREE FROM SIN'S GRIME

The Spirit also liberates us from the control and lingering effects of sin. A big part of the Holy Spirit's job description is to set every believer apart for God as someone holy. For all your Christian life on this earth, the Spirit will be at work to detach you from any dependence on whatever is unlike God. You're being made holy, just as the Spirit Himself is holy.

This process is called sanctification. The Bible says we're "sanctified by the Holy Spirit" (Romans 15:16). We're chosen of God through "the sanctifying work of the Spirit" (1 Peter 1:2, NIV).

You were an ugly caterpillar before, slimy and slow, but never again.

It's all part of the Spirit's cleanup work in our lives. In fact, you've already been soaked and scrubbed: "You were washed, you were sanctified...by the Spirit of our God" (1 Corinthians 6:11).

My wife loves to keep a spotlessly clean home, but there's one cleaning job she despises—scouring the bathtub.

When we got married, she asked me nicely if I would always take care of that particular chore (along with taking out the trash), and I agreed. Whenever we were moving, I looked for places that had only showers, but we've had our share of tubs as well. And cleaning them is no fun. I'm on my knees and I'm hunching over the tub, very uncomfortable, and I've got to scrub and rinse and then scrub some more and rinse some more—because although she didn't want to clean it, she does want to inspect it. So I had to work hard.

But as the years went by, I noticed in the store one day a new cleaning product for tubs. I just spray it on, and it penetrates the dirt. The grime just bubbles and foams up, then all I have to do is wipe it off.

Too many of us are hunched down on our knees trying to scrub the dirty mess out of our lives: *I'm trying, I'm trying; it's so hard, but I'm trying!*

The Holy Spirit is here to tell you that He's got the cleaner that's perfectly designed to do that work for you. If you simply apply walking in the Spirit in your spiritual life, He'll bubble up the mess inside you so that all you have to do is wipe it clean, not scrub it out. All you have to do is take advantage of what He's already done, because God has cleaned us "by the washing of regeneration and renewal of the Holy Spirit" (Titus 3:5).

No Longer Under Law

Our liberation in the Spirit also means that we're free from the law. "If you are led by the Spirit," the Bible says, "you are not under the law" (Galatians 5:18). This is made possible because of the loving relationship we now enjoy with God through the Spirit, a relationship that is vastly higher than law.

Picture in your mind a newlywed couple. The young wife happily cooks meals and cleans house for her husband, even though no rule was ever stated; he never said, "You've got to cook for me and clean for me." She does it gladly and voluntarily because of her relationship with him.

Now jump ahead ten years. The relationship has gotten rocky. The wife still cooks and cleans, but it's no longer a joy to her. It's a duty. It's a rule. It's a law.

Where the relationship is weak or lacking, you must function by law. But where the relationship is strong and loving and growing, you can be performing the same duties and yet do them gladly and enjoyably, without any law.

> Where the relationship is weak or lacking, you must function by law.

Whenever you see Christians living by their lists—

don't do this, don't do that, don't go here, don't go there, *don't, don't, don't*—you're seeing Christians who haven't yet learned to walk by the Spirit.

So if you want to get away from the misery of having a long list to follow in the Christian life—as you grit your teeth and tell yourself, "I've got to do this because I'm a Christian and I'm supposed to do it"—then know that all you need to do is cultivate your relationship with the Spirit.

FAR BEYOND THE RULES

The fact is, though the law itself is good, all it can realistically accomplish in your life is condemnation. On its own, it cannot help you.

It's like a traffic officer on patrol. Have you ever been pulled over by a law officer who congratulated you for driving within the speed limit? He tells you, "I just wanted to let you know that the limit here is seventy, and you were holding at sixty-nine, and I deeply appreciate it." Nope, I don't doubt that's happened to you. Instead, that patrolman is waiting to catch you there doing eighty or eighty-five, so he can stop you and initiate unpleasant consequences.

The law is like your bathroom mirror. It shows how you look every morning, but you don't then take the mirror off the wall and comb your hair with it or shave with it or use it to put on your makeup. The law can show you what's wrong, but it can't fix it.

Only the Spirit can actually fix us—and as He does it, He gives us the full freedom of a relationship with God that far surpasses any rules.

Chapter 8

THE LIGHT OF HIS GUIDANCE

If Jesus were here on earth today, and in fact living right in your own home, who would be the first person you turned to when facing a problem in your life? Of course it would be Jesus. You wouldn't phone up your pastor first, or a Christian psychiatrist—not if you could step right into the room where Jesus is and sit down and talk with Him.

You may have thought many times, *If only I lived back in Jesus' day!* Or, *If only Jesus were physically here in our day, I know I could handle life so much better.*

But the reality is that we have a situation far better than that. And Jesus Himself was careful to explain why.

LEFT BEHIND

On the night before He would be crucified, Jesus talked with His disciples about leaving them. This was no small matter to them. The One whom they had risked their lives for and left their jobs and families for was now saying, "I'm leaving." It prompted a fundamental question in their minds: How are we supposed to manage if You're not here? We have enough trouble making it while You *are* here; how will we ever pull through if You leave us behind?

Their question is very much our question as well, as we try to follow Jesus in our troubling world. How do we really do it when He's not here?

That same night, Jesus talked much about the Holy Spirit to His disciples. "I will ask the Father," He promised, "and he will give you another Helper, to be with you forever" (John 14:16). A short while later He added, "It is to your advantage that I go away, for if I do not go away, the Helper will not come to you. But if I go, I will send him to you" (16:7).

This word for "Helper" is the Greek word *parakletos,* which means "someone called alongside to assist." Jesus had always been the disciples' Helper before; and now, even after He left them, they would still have His help, His guidance, His encouragement—all through the Holy Spirit. "You know him," Jesus said, "for he dwells with you and will be in you" (14:17).

Jesus was telling them, "This Helper, this Holy Spirit, will be to you exactly what I have been to you." By having the Holy Spirit, they would have nothing less than they had with Jesus.

That's also the way it is with us. In fact, if Jesus were still here on earth in human form, we would be worse off as Christians. Our lives would be horrible—we would be miserable, hopeless, defeated, discouraged, disgusted.

That's because when Jesus walked on earth, the presence of His deity was always limited to His physical location. He was always God, but He was the God-man, so

> If Jesus were still here on earth in human form, we would be worse off as Christians.

that receiving His direct ministry was contingent upon a connection with His physical, human presence. And He could only be in one place at one time. But with the Holy Spirit, Jesus can be everywhere all at once. All of us can have Him, wherever we happen to be.

Nobody loses in this Holy Spirit deal!

SOMETHING YOU NEED TO KNOW

Probably the most practical way we experience our Helper's presence is in the guidance and intervention He continues to give us. The more you depend on the Spirit of God, the more you'll be guided.

My own call to the ministry and to the proclamation of God's Word came this way. While I was reading Paul's statement, "Woe is unto me, if I preach not the gospel!" (1 Corinthians 9:16, KJV), the Holy Spirit caused those words to jump off the pages of Scripture into my heart. I knew the voice of God was personally calling me into vocational Christian ministry.

On another occasion my wife witnessed a very different kind of intervention from the Spirit. As she was driving to her office one morning, she remembered that she'd left her lunch at home. She decided to go back and get it.

When she walked through the door, she was shocked to hear blaring alarms and to see the house filling with smoke.

It turned out that a heating element in the ceiling of an upstairs bathroom had fallen onto a pile of clothes and ignited them. The nearby cabinets were already on fire. If she hadn't gone back, or if she'd delayed even fifteen minutes, the whole house might well have been destroyed.

After firefighters extinguished the blaze, one of them said to Lois, "Lady, you sure must be close to God." Yes, God was close to my wife that morning. The thought in her mind about her lunch left behind was the Spirit's way of telling her, "Turn around. There's something you need to know about."

Many of us often confront even worse threats and dangers in our lives, and we need God's hand to help us face them. Meanwhile, even in everyday life we encounter a constant stream of decisions and demands—so many choices, concerns, opportunities, needs. Sometimes you don't know which way to turn. You need guidance, and that's exactly what the Spirit supplies. He offers to steer you in the will of God, to navigate your life for you.

The Holy Spirit is like a GPS (Global Positioning System) device that lets us know exactly where we are. His purpose is to be the voice of God in our hearts to direct us through the twists and turns of life in accordance with the Word and will of God.

That's why going to someone else for counsel before you go to the Spirit of God is like rubbing first aid cream on a broken leg. It may feel a little better for the moment, but your problem hasn't been solved. The Spirit needs to be our first contact point as we seek Him in prayer and in God's Word.

And when you do go to people for counsel, you want to make sure they're full of the Holy Spirit, so their spiritual abundance can be applied to your own spiritual need. Their filling will be evidenced by counsel based on the Word of God, and their passion will be to move you in line with the will of God. When this is present, there will be an inner witness between you and that person.

HEARING THE SPIRIT'S VOICE

To hear the Spirit's guidance, we have to grow in learning to hear His "voice"—which we also call the witness of the Spirit. It's when the objective Word of God and your subjective human spirit are linked by the revealing and confirming work of the Holy Spirit, and the meaning and application of the Word hits you in a real and powerful way. He takes the still photographs of God's words and turns them into a motion picture of your own life. You understand what decisions He wants you to make and what actions He wants you to take.

Now the Word of God is the Word of God whether or not it "hits" you like this. But when it comes to guidance, you need it to hit you. You need to know how God's Word applies to your daily circumstances. You need His illumination—where He turns the lightbulb on—as you look at those words on the pages of your Bible.

It's like the difference between a simple store-bought pregnancy test—where a woman puts the little slip of paper into a solution, and it tells her if she's pregnant—and a doctor's ultrasound examination that actually shows the baby moving. One is just information; the other is a picture of life.

The Holy Spirit will take what's on paper in the Bible and animate it for us in a picture we see with the eyes of our heart. The message becomes real, dynamic—alive in our understanding and our experience.

He wants this to happen for us again and again, so that He's constantly renewing our minds and we begin to think like God thinks. We see things increasingly from His vantage point. The Spirit helps us grasp more and more what God wants to do in our lives.

Maybe the Bible doesn't seem alive to you. You believe it, you know it's true, but you just don't sense the power of it. The Holy Spirit's role is somehow being hindered in your experience.

Paul tells us we have received the Spirit "that we may understand what God has freely given us"; he says that whatever is given us, "God has revealed it to us by his Spirit"; and whatever is revealed includes truly amazing things, for "no eye has seen, no ear has heard, no mind has conceived what God has prepared for those who love him" (1 Corinthians 2:9–12, NIV).

To receive this amazing revelation from the Spirit, you've got to cultivate your relationship with Him. If you keep Him in the background and let other things crowd Him out, it's like trying to talk on the phone while the TV is turned up loud; you just won't hear Him. You've got to cut down those distractions and lower the volume on the other noises in your life. That's why Jesus often said, "He who has an ear, let him hear."

WHEN BIBLE TEACHING MAKES YOU WORSE

Be aware that it's possible to hear the Bible and not hear the Lord. People hear the Word of God preached and make sincere commitments to obey it only to discover three days later that they've gone right back to where they were before. In fact, you can actually listen to Bible teaching and be worse off than before. You can sit under Bible teaching and actually regress— becoming a worse Christian instead of a better one.

> You can sit under Bible teaching and actually regress— becoming worse instead of better.

If that's a curve ball for you, let me explain with an example from my own life. When I went to seminary, I was full of excitement at the thought of learning from some of the best Bible teachers of that time. This particular seminary is considered one of the greatest Bible-teaching institutions in the world, with a reputation as a place where a student will definitely learn the Word of God.

From morning till night I delved into the Bible. Over the course of those years I studied not only every book in the Bible, but also theology—the doctrines of the Bible. I studied apologetics—how to defend the Bible. I studied Hebrew and Greek—the original languages of the Bible.

But every year I was in seminary, I drifted farther from the faith. I began to get cold. I got so into the truth of what I was learning that it became mere information. I was memorizing information to pass examinations, but there was no transformation occurring, no change of life— because that comes only through the Spirit.

Some Christians look at the problems in their churches and say, "What we need is more Bible." Well, maybe that's not the problem. Maybe they have plenty of Bible, and what they really need more of is the Spirit's filling.

Now don't misunderstand me. You absolutely need the Bible. The Bible is critical, foundational—but it must be animated by the Spirit of God. Whenever the Bible becomes an end in itself, then it's only information rather than the path to transformation. But when we have Bible-centeredness combined with the filling of the Spirit, we get to see the supernatural hand of God at work.

Never Alone

Because of the Holy Spirit's witness and illumination, you never have to be alone in your decisions—but this is true only as long as you're seeking the mind of God and wanting to do His will. If you're determined to do your own will, the light will stay off. The Holy Spirit will not even reveal His will if you're already committed to your own selfish plans.

To see His clear guidance, you must decide in advance that you're going to obey whatever He reveals. If that's your passion—if you say, "Lord, whatever You want me to do, I'll do it"—then He will assuredly be your personal Illuminator.

Chapter 9

GOD'S POWER FOR
GOD'S WORK

One summer I drove my family to the Grand Canyon for a vacation. If you've gone there, you know there are only a couple of lodging establishments anywhere near it; and on this occasion, I had failed to make reservations.

We arrived at eleven o'clock at night, and as I walked into the hotel lobby, I saw a line of tired and irritated people at the front desk. The thought struck me at once: *There's no room for us.*

As the twenty or so people in line were turned away one by one, my turn came to step forward and ask for a room.

"Well," the man behind the desk said, "as you heard me say to the people in front of you, all our rooms are taken, and the closest hotel we can book you in is an hour and a half away."

So we weren't happy campers, and my family wasn't real excited about my leadership on this occasion.

After all those hours on the road, we went to the restroom to wash up, then sat down in the hotel restaurant to have something to eat while we decided whether to sleep in our van or hit the road again.

As we sat around the table, one of my daughters looked up and said, "But Daddy, you haven't prayed!"

I didn't want to hear that. At the moment, I preferred to hear something practical—like who was going to volunteer to take my place behind the wheel for the next hour and a half. So I looked at her and said, "You pray."

And she did, in her sweet way: "Lord, we don't have a room, and we're too tired to go anywhere. Would you give us a room? Amen."

> She looked up and said, "But Daddy, you haven't prayed!"

Then it was time to get practical. What were we going to do? While we discussed it over dinner, the man from behind the front desk came walking through the restaurant. He paused at our table and asked, "Weren't you one of the parties looking for a room?"

I said, "Yes."

He explained that a family that was checked in had to leave unexpectedly because of an emergency. "There are no other people in line—would you still like a room?"

I couldn't help exchanging glances with my daughter. As far as we were concerned, this was nothing short of a miraculous intervention from God.

ARE YOU SEEING MIRACLES?

God still does miracles today. He saves somebody who looked unsavable; He restores a marriage that was shattered beyond repair; He breaks habits that couldn't be broken; He creates lasting changes in someone we've been praying for and who seemed likely never to change.

God still does all that. But if you aren't getting to know the Holy Spirit, you'll miss having a part in it.

Unfortunately, some of us in the church have reacted wrongly to what we perceive as excesses among other believers in their emphasis on the miraculous—and it's caused some of us to miss the main point. We should be seeing many more miracles in our lives than we're seeing, but because we haven't majored on the Spirit like He needs to be majored on, we miss out on His miracles. Many of us no longer even expect them.

Now the Holy Spirit doesn't do miracles just for the miracles' sake. That's the problem with people who think of the Spirit as a power more than as the person He truly is. They just want to get the next goodie from God, miraculously.

Jesus promised the Spirit's power only as it related to accomplishing our God-given work in the kingdom of God. If you want His kingdom power, you must be living for His kingdom purposes. You can't be dually aligned—living as much for this world as you are for the world to come—and expect to see His miraculous power. He doesn't do joint ventures and limited partnerships. God wants it all. He has to be in charge; He has to be the dictator of your existence.

INTERVENTION

When He's fully in charge, you can expect to see His intervention. You'll see Him stepping into the natural realm with His supernatural presence.

> The Holy Spirit
> doesn't do
> miracles just
> for the
> miracles' sake.

A little thing happened to me the other day. I was leaving home in a hurry to drive to an important meeting, but I couldn't find my car keys. After searching several minutes, I stopped in the den and sat down.

"Lord," I said, "because of the nature of this meeting and because of its kingdom implications, unless You don't want me to get there, I need You to intervene. I don't have the slightest idea where my keys are, but You know."

After praying, I stayed seated for a moment as I mentally developed a methodical plan for what I should do next. Once I had my plan, I started to stand up, and I placed my hands on the couch beside me. My fingers slid between the cushions, and I heard a jingle.

There were my keys.

God intervenes!

POWER FOR A PURPOSE

And when God intervenes, it's to make sure we have the power we need for accomplishing His purposes.

There's probably no greater statement about the Spirit's power than what we find in a verse most believers learn early in their Christian life. It's a promise Jesus gave His disciples just before He ascended to heaven. He told them, "You will receive power when the Holy Spirit has come upon you, and you will be my witnesses" (Acts 1:8). Jesus was saying, "You'll indeed bear witness of Me—but only when you get the power...which comes only from the dynamite of the Holy Spirit."

Now these disciples had spent three years listening to Jesus—three years of going to "seminary," three years of being taught by the eternal Son of God. They were not lacking information. They were not lacking a good Bible teacher. They were not lacking instruction on what God wanted them to do. But Jesus knew the one thing they were lacking—power. And He told them that until the Holy Spirit came, they would not experience such power. Their knowledge wouldn't work for them. It would only be gray information, seemingly unreal. He told them to wait for the Holy Spirit to come upon them...and they did wait.

THE INVASION

On the day of Pentecost, their comfortable surroundings were shaken—the Spirit came with a violent wind and tongues of flame, a powerful invasion from heaven like nothing they'd ever known before. "And they were all filled with the Holy Spirit" (Acts 2:4). God was setting them apart as the church to get full of the Spirit so they had power to pull off everything the Lord Jesus had taught them.

What we see in the rest of the book of Acts is the outworking of this new and mighty dynamic of a Spirit-empowered church. In Acts we see believers both individually and corporately filled with the

> Jesus knew the one thing they were lacking—power.

Spirit, and it made all the difference in the world for the church: "They were all filled with the Holy Spirit and continued to speak the word of God with boldness" (4:31). They walked "in the fear of the Lord and in the comfort of the Holy Spirit" (9:31). They "were filled with joy and with the Holy Spirit" (13:52). They were able to walk and talk in a way they never could before—all because of the Holy Spirit.

The book of Acts is all about what the church looks like when the Holy Spirit takes over. And the greatest thing that can be said about any local church today is that it's filled with people who are full of the Holy Spirit, ready to do His work.

SPIRITUAL GIFTS

How does the Holy Spirit equip us for His work? By providing spiritual gifts—supernatural abilities, sensitivities, and inclinations that empower believers to build up the body, overcome obstacles, and press on to success.

Some believers seem to talk about "my spiritual gift" as if it's some kind of merit badge for their spirituality. But we discover in Scripture that there's no necessary correlation between spirituality and spiritual gifts. Even worldly believers can exercise spiritual gifts, because the spiritually gifted Corinthian church was immature, "still of the flesh"

(1 Corinthians 3:3). Their church was carnal and chaotic, yet they evidenced a proliferation of spiritual gifts. To be truly spiritual, you must be filled by the Spirit and walking in the Spirit, not just exercising a spiritual gift.

When Paul teaches us about the Spirit's gifts for all believers, he sums it up this way: "To each is given the manifestation of the Spirit for the common good" (12:7). There are two big factors here that we often overlook.

About Him, Not You

Notice first that a spiritual gift is *not* merely a demonstration of your own natural abilities or talents, but a "manifestation of the Spirit." They're about Him, not about you.

When I was just a boy in junior high school, I stuttered profusely. I had to attend special speech classes to help me try to get over it. I was terrible at talking—*except when I talked about Jesus.* When I spoke about Jesus, my stammering tongue cleared up. My abilities were transformed; there was a manifestation of the Spirit.

Even today I sometimes have a recurring lisp, and I'm reminded of how bad it used to be. So whatever blessing has come to others through my preaching ministry is because of a manifestation of the Spirit and not because of the speaking ability of Tony Evans, because my tongue was a stammering tongue.

THE GAUGE

The second big factor to notice in Paul's summary statement about spiritual gifts is that their purpose is to benefit the body of Christ—"for the common good." You know that it's a true spiritual gift when it's a blessing to other believers and not just something for yourself. As Peter says, "As each has received a gift, *use it to serve one another,* as good stewards of God's varied grace" (1 Peter 4:10).

In reality, you cannot develop true intimacy with the Spirit without also developing intimacy with the other members of God's family through loving service to them. You cannot have fellowship with the Spirit if you're out of fellowship with the family. This is a fundamental principle that we often miss.

> You cannot have fellowship with the Spirit if you're out of fellowship with God's family.

When I was in elementary school in Baltimore, one day I stuck my head in the boiler room and happened to notice a little gauge on the boiler that heated the building. I asked the custodian what it was. He showed me the lines on the gauge and explained that the level of water inside it was an indication of how much water was in the boiler. "The boiler's too hot to open and check it there," he said, "so we check it here."

Our love and service toward our brothers and sisters in Christ is the gauge for our own spirituality and for how much we truly love and serve God. We measure the unseen by the seen.

DON'T LOOK FOR YOUR SPIRITUAL GIFT

So we can define a spiritual gift as a divinely bestowed ability to serve the body of Christ.

You may now be asking, "So how do I find out my spiritual gift?"

Let me say first how you *don't* find it out. You don't discover it by looking for it. I disagree with these "gift surveys" that some Christians promote. There's no command in the Bible to "find your spiritual gift." So you can stop looking for it now.

But you say, "How can I use it if I don't look for it and find it?"

The answer is simple. In the Bible, when God revealed gifts, it came in conjunction with a task. When God calls you to a task, He also provides the supernatural ability to accomplish it. Your gifts will emerge as you carry out the work He assigns you. And when He calls you to another task that demands a different ability, He'll supply another gift for it. If He changes your task, He also changes or adapts your gifts. And their purpose is not so you can go around telling others, "I have this gift." Their purpose is simply to accomplish His work with His power in His way.

So look for God's task, not for your gift. As you start to carry out the task, His gift will be manifested.

EVERY ANGLE COVERED

Do you see how when it comes to getting God's work done for God's kingdom, He has every angle covered? Through the Holy Spirit, He provides us with specific guidance about the task, plus the motivation, the enabling power, and the specific tools (His gifts) to accomplish it.

All that remains is for us to be willing to get to work…as we keep on being filled with the Spirit and walking confidently in full reliance upon Him.

Let the Spirit come alongside you now in every responsibility and issue you face in life. Let Him enliven the words of Scripture and show you exactly what God wants you to do. Commit to doing what He shows you and be ready and trusting to receive His enabling and giftedness to accomplish it.

And be watching…as He ignites your life with a transforming fire.

The publisher and author would love to hear your comments about this book. *Please contact us at:*
www.lifechangebooks.com

THE URBAN ALTERNATIVE